Train up a child in the way he should go,
and when he is old he
will not depart from it.

—

Proverbs 22:6 NKJV

20 THINGS

I NEED TO TELL MY SON

The quoted ideas expressed in this book (but not Scripture verses) are not, in all cases, exact quotations, as some have been edited for clarity and brevity. In all cases, the author has attempted to maintain the speaker's original intent. In some cases, quoted material for this book was obtained from secondary sources, primarily print media. While every effort was made to ensure the accuracy of these sources, the accuracy cannot be guaranteed. For additions, deletions, corrections, or clarifications in future editions of this text, please write Freeman-Smith, LLC.

The Holy Bible, King James Version

The Holy Bible, New King James Version (NKJV) Copyright © 1982 by Thomas Nelson, Inc. Used by permission.

New Century Version®. (NCV) Copyright © 1987, 1988, 1991 by Word Publishing, a division of Thomas Nelson, Inc. All rights reserved. Used by permission.

The Holman Christian Standard Bible™ (Holman CSB) Copyright © 1999, 2000, 2001 by Holman Bible Publishers. Used by permission.

The Holy Bible, New International Version®. (NIV) Copyright © 1973, 1978, 1984 International Bible Society. Used by permission of Zondervan. All rights reserved.

The Holy Bible. New Living Translation (NLT) copyright © 1996 Tyndale Charitable Trust. Used by permission of Tyndale House Publishers.

The New American Standard Bible®, (NASB) Copyright © 1960, 1962, 1963, 1968, 1971, 1972, 1973, 1975, 1977, 1995 by The Lockman Foundation. Used by permission.

Scripture taken from The Message. (MSG) Copyright © 1993, 1994, 1995, 1996, 2000, 2001, 2002. Used by permission of NavPress Publishing Group.

Cover Design by Kim Russell / Wahoo Designs
Page Layout by Bart Dawson

ISBN 978-1-60587-109-7

Printed in the United States of America

20 THINGS
I NEED TO TELL MY SON

Devotions to Strengthen Your Relationship

INDEX OF TOPICS

INTRODUCTION

A MESSAGE TO PARENTS

Because you're older and wiser than your son, you have much to teach him (even if he doesn't think so). But what lessons should you teach first? After all, you probably have hundreds of ideas rattling around in your brain, all of them important. And with so many things to consider, you may have found it tough to organize your thoughts. So, perhaps you haven't yet taken the time to sit down with your son and share your own personalized set of life-lessons in a systematic way. If that's the case, this book can help.

This text focuses on 20 timeless insights for Christians, lessons that your son desperately needs to hear from you. So here's your assignment: read this book, add your own personal insights in the back, and then schedule a series of face-to-face, no-interruptions-allowed, parent-to-son talks with the young guy whom God has entrusted to your care. Carve out enough time to really explore these concepts, and don't be afraid to share your own personal experiences: your victories, your defeats, and the lessons you learned along the way.

We live in a world where far too many parents have out-sourced the job of raising their kids, with predictably sour results. And make no mistake, your youngster is going to learn about life from somebody; in fact, he's learning about life every single day—some of the lessons are positive, and quite a few aren't. So ask yourself: Is your boy being tutored by the world or by you? The world will, at times, intentionally mislead your youngster, but you never will. So grab this book, grab your notes, grab your boy, and have the kind of parent-to-son talks that both of you deserve.

GOD HAS A PLAN FOR YOUR LIFE THAT'S BIGGER (AND BETTER) THAN YOURS.

"For I know the plans I have for you"
—[this is] the Lord's declaration—
"plans for [your] welfare, not for disaster,
to give you a future and a hope."

—

Jeremiah 29:11 Holman CSB

Talk to Your Son About God's Plan

The Bible makes it clear: God has plans—very big plans—for you and your family. But He won't force His plans upon you—if you wish to experience the abundance that God has in store, you must be willing to accept His will and follow His Son.

As Christians, you and your family members should ask yourselves this question: "How closely can we make our plans match God's plans?" The more closely you manage to follow the path that God intends for your lives, the better.

Your son undoubtedly has concerns about his present circumstances, and you should encourage him to take those concerns to God in prayer. Your son has hopes and dreams. You should encourage him to talk to God about those dreams. And your son is making plans for the future, a future by the way, that only the Creator can see. You should ask your youngster to let God guide his steps.

So remember that God intends to use you—and your son—in wonderful, unexpected ways. And it's up to you to seek His plan for your own life while encouraging your son to do the same. When you do, you'll discover that God's plans are grand and glorious . . . more glorious than either of you can imagine.

*We know that all things work together
for the good of those who love God:
those who are called according
to His purpose.*

—

Romans 8:28 Holman CSB

More from God's Word About God's Guidance

I will instruct you and show you the way to go; with My eye on you, I will give counsel.

Psalm 32:8 Holman CSB

For as many as are led by the Spirit of God, they are the sons of God.

Romans 8:14 KJV

Lord, You light my lamp; my God illuminates my darkness.

Psalm 18:28 Holman CSB

In all your ways acknowledge Him, and He shall direct your paths.

Proverbs 3:6 NKJV

He awakens [Me] each morning; He awakens My ear to listen like those being instructed. The Lord God has opened My ear, and I was not rebellious; I did not turn back.

Isaiah 50:4-5 Holman CSB

MORE GREAT IDEAS

It's incredible to realize that what we do each day has meaning in the big picture of God's plan.

Bill Hybels

God has a plan for the life of every Christian. Every circumstance, every turn of destiny, all things work together for your good and for His glory.

Billy Graham

If not a sparrow falls upon the ground without your Father, you have reason to see that the smallest events of your career and your life are arranged by him.

C. H. Spurgeon

God has a course mapped out for your life, and all the inadequacies in the world will not change His mind. He will be with you every step of the way. And though it may take time, He has a celebration planned for when you cross over the "Red Seas" of your life.

Charles Swindoll

Our heavenly Father never takes anything from his children unless he means to give them something better.

George Mueller

I thought God's purpose was to make me full of happiness and joy. It is, but it is happiness and joy from God's standpoint, not from mine.

Oswald Chambers

If you believe in a God who controls the big things, you have to believe in a God who controls the little things. It is we, of course, to whom things look "little" or "big."

Elisabeth Elliot

I don't doubt that the Holy Spirit guides your decisions from within when you make them with the intention of pleasing God. The error would be to think that He speaks only within, whereas in reality He speaks also through Scripture, the Church, Christian friends, and books.

C. S. Lewis

POINTS OF EMPHASIS:
Write Down at Least Three Things About God's Plan That Your Son Needs to Hear from You:

_____

_____

_____

_____

_____

_____

_____

_____

_____

_____

_____

_____

_____

_____

A TIME TO PRAY:
Write Down Your Prayer for Your Son about This Chapter:

Dear Lord,

_____

_____

_____

_____

_____

_____

_____

_____

_____

_____

_____

_____

_____

_____

Amen

PRAYER IS MORE POWERFUL THAN YOU THINK, SO IF YOU NEED SOMETHING, ASK GOD.

*So I say to you, keep asking,
and it will be given to you. Keep searching,
and you will find. Keep knocking,
and the door will be opened to you.*

–

Luke 11:9 Holman CSB

Talk to Your Son About Prayer

Genuine, heartfelt prayer produces powerful changes in us and in our world. When we lift our hearts to God, we open ourselves to a never-ending source of divine wisdom and infinite love. So as a Christian parent, you must make certain that your child understands the power of prayer and the need for prayer. And the best way to do so, of course, is by example.

Is prayer an integral part of your family's life, or is it a hit-or-miss habit? Do you "pray without ceasing," or is your prayer life an afterthought? Do you regularly honor God in the solitude of the early morning darkness, or do you bow your head only when others are watching?

The quality of your son's spiritual life will be in direct proportion to the quality of his prayer life. Prayer changes things, and it will change him. So when you can tell he's turning things over in his mind, encourage him to turn them over to God in prayer. And while you're at it, don't limit your family's prayers to meals or to bedtime. Make sure that your family is constantly praying about things great and small because God is listening, and He wants to hear from you now.

*Verily, verily, I say unto you,
He that believeth on me, the works that
I do shall he do also; and greater works than these
shall he do; because I go unto my Father.
And whatsoever ye shall ask in my name,
that will I do, that the Father may be glorified
in the Son. If ye shall ask any thing in my name,
I will do it.*

—

John 14:12-14 KJV

More from God's Word About
Prayer

The intense prayer of the righteous is very powerful.

James 5:16 Holman CSB

Let the words of my mouth and the meditation of my heart be acceptable in Your sight, O Lord, my strength and my Redeemer.

Psalm 19:14 NKJV

Yet He often withdrew to deserted places and prayed.

Luke 5:16 Holman CSB

Don't worry about anything, but in everything, through prayer and petition with thanksgiving, let your requests be made known to God.

Philippians 4:6 Holman CSB

Rejoice in hope; be patient in affliction; be persistent in prayer.

Romans 12:12 Holman CSB

MORE GREAT IDEAS

Some people think God does not like to be troubled with our constant asking. But, the way to trouble God is not to come at all.

D. L. Moody

If you want more from life, ask more from God.

Criswell Freeman

Notice that we must ask. And we will sometimes struggle to hear and struggle with what we hear. But personally, it's worth it. I'm after the path of life—and he alone knows it.

John Eldredge

God's help is always available, but it is only given to those who seek it.

Max Lucado

Don't be afraid to ask your heavenly Father for anything you need. Indeed, nothing is too small for God's attention or too great for his power.

Dennis Swanberg

God will help us become the people we are meant to be, if only we will ask Him.

Hannah Whitall Smith

We honor God by asking for great things
when they are a part of His promise.
We dishonor Him and cheat ourselves
when we ask for molehills
where He has promised mountains.

—

Vance Havner

POINTS OF EMPHASIS:
Write Down at Least Three Things About Asking God
That Your Son Needs to Hear from You:

_____

_____

_____

_____

_____

_____

_____

_____

_____

_____

_____

_____

_____

_____

A Time to Pray:
Write Down Your Prayer for Your Son about This Chapter:

Dear Lord,

_____

_____

_____

_____

_____

_____

_____

_____

_____

_____

_____

_____

_____

Amen

WITH FAITH, YOU CAN MOVE MOUNTAINS, WITHOUT FAITH, YOU CAN'T.

I assure you: If anyone says to this mountain,
"Be lifted up and thrown into the sea,"
and does not doubt in his heart,
but believes that what he says will happen,
it will be done for him.

–

Mark 11:23 Holman CSB

Talk to Your Son About
Faith

Because we live in a demanding world, all of us, parents and children alike, have mountains to climb and mountains to move. Moving those mountains requires faith. And the experience of trying, with God's help, to move mountains builds character.

Faith, like a tender seedling, can be nurtured or neglected. When we nurture our faith through prayer, meditation, and worship, God blesses our lives and lifts our spirits. But when we fail to consult the Father early and often, we do ourselves and our loved ones a profound disservice.

Are you a mountain-moving person whose faith is evident for your son to see? Or, are you a spiritual shrinking violet? As you think about the answer to that question, consider this: God needs more people—and especially more parents—who are willing to move mountains for His glory and for His kingdom.

Every life—including your son's life—is a series of wins and losses. Every step of the way, through every triumph and every trial, God walks with your child, ready and willing to strengthen him. So the next time your son's character is being tested, remind him to take his concerns to God. And while you're at it, remind your youngster that no problem is too big for Creator of the universe.

With God, all things are possible, and He stands ready to open a world of possibilities to your son and to you . . . if you have faith. So, with no further ado, let the mountain-moving begin.

———◆◆———

If you do not stand firm in your faith,
then you will not stand at all.

—

Isaiah 7:9 Holman CSB

*For we walk by faith,
not by sight.*

—

2 Corinthians 5:7 Holman CSB

MORE FROM GOD'S WORD ABOUT WORSHIP

I rejoiced with those who said to me, "Let us go to the house of the Lord."

Psalm 122:1 Holman CSB

But an hour is coming, and is now here, when the true worshipers will worship the Father in spirit and truth. Yes, the Father wants such people to worship Him. God is Spirit, and those who worship Him must worship in spirit and truth.

John 4:23-24 Holman CSB

For where two or three are gathered together in My name, I am there among them.

Matthew 18:20 Holman CSB

So that at the name of Jesus every knee should bow—of those who are in heaven and on earth and under the earth—and every tongue should confess that Jesus Christ is Lord, to the glory of God the Father.

Philippians 2:10-11 Holman CSB

MORE GREAT IDEAS

There are a lot of things in life that are difficult to understand. Faith allows the soul to go beyond what the eyes can see.

John Maxwell

The popular idea of faith is of a certain obstinate optimism: the hope, tenaciously held in the face of trouble, that the universe is fundamentally friendly and things may get better.

J. I. Packer

I am truly grateful that faith enables me to move past the question of "Why?"

Zig Ziglar

When you enroll in the "school of faith," you never know what may happen next. The life of faith presents challenges that keep you going—and keep you growing!

Warren Wiersbe

Faith's wings are clipped by reason's scissors.

R. G. Lee

Faith is to believe
what you do not see;
the reward of this faith
is to see what you believe.

—

St. Augustine

POINTS OF EMPHASIS:
Write Down at Least Three Things About Faith That
Your Son Needs to Hear from You:

_____

_____

_____

_____

_____

_____

_____

_____

_____

_____

_____

_____

_____

_____

A TIME TO PRAY:
Write Down Your Prayer for Your Son about This Chapter:

Dear Lord,

_____

_____

_____

_____

_____

_____

_____

_____

_____

_____

_____

_____

_____

_____

Amen

IT'S MORE IMPORTANT TO BE RIGHT THAN TO BE POPULAR.

*Flee from youthful passions, and pursue
righteousness, faith, love, and peace,
along with those who call on the Lord
from a pure heart.*

—

2 Timothy 2:22 Holman CSB

TALK TO YOUR SON ABOUT
DOING WHAT'S RIGHT

If your son is like most young men, he will seek the admiration of his friends and classmates. But the eagerness to please others should never overshadow his eagerness to please God. God has big plans for your son, and if your youngster intends to fulfill God's plans by following God's Son, then your son must seek to please the Father first and always.

Everyday life is an adventure in decision-making. Each day, your youngster will make countless decisions that will hopefully bring him closer to God. When your son obeys God's commandments, he inevitably experiences God's abundance and His peace. But, if your youngster turns his back on God by disobeying Him, your youngster will unintentionally invite Old Man Trouble to stop by for an extended visit.

Do you want your child to be successful and happy? Then encourage him to study God's Word and live by it.

If your son follows that advice, then when he faces a difficult choice or a powerful temptation (which he most certainly will), he'll be prepared to meet the enemy head-on.

So, as a thoughtful parent, your task is straightforward: encourage your child to seek God's approval in every aspect of his life. Does this sound too simple? Perhaps it is simple, but it is also the only way for your youngster to reap the marvelous riches that God has in store for him.

———◆———

For the eyes of the Lord are over the righteous,
and his ears are open unto their prayers:
but the face of the Lord
is against them that do evil.

—

1 Peter 3:12 KJV

MORE FROM GOD'S WORD ABOUT OBEDIENCE TO GOD

Walk in wisdom toward outsiders, making the most of the time.

Colossians 4:5 Holman CSB

Let us not lose heart in doing good, for in due time we shall reap if we do not grow weary. So then, while we have opportunity, let us do good to all men, and especially to those who are of the household of the faith.

Galatians 6:9-10 NASB

Consider it a great joy, my brothers, whenever you experience various trials, knowing that the testing of your faith produces endurance. But endurance must do its complete work, so that you may be mature and complete, lacking nothing.

James 1:2-4 Holman CSB

Blessed are the pure in heart, because they will see God.

Matthew 5:8 Holman CSB

But seek first the kingdom of God and His righteousness, and all these things will be provided for you.

Matthew 6:33 Holman CSB

MORE GREAT IDEAS

Impurity is not just a wrong action; impurity is the state of mind and heart and soul which is just the opposite of purity and wholeness.

A. W. Tozer

Righteousness not only defines God, but God defines righteousness.

Bill Hybels

Have your heart right with Christ, and he will visit you often, and so turn weekdays into Sundays, meals into sacraments, homes into temples, and earth into heaven.

C. H. Spurgeon

What is God looking for? He is looking for men and women whose hearts are completely His.

Charles Swindoll

Holiness is not the way to Jesus—Jesus is the way to holiness.

Anonymous

The great thing is to be found at one's post as a child of God, living each day as though it were our last, but planning as though our world might last a hundred years.

C. S. Lewis

Learning God's truth and getting it into our heads is one thing, but living God's truth and getting it into our characters is quite something else.

Warren Wiersbe

Nobody is good by accident. No man ever became holy by chance.

C. H. Spurgeon

Many of the difficulties that we experience as Christians can be traced to a lack of Bible study. We should not be content to skim the Bible. We must place the Word of God in our hearts!

Billy Graham

POINTS OF EMPHASIS:
Write Down at Least Three Things About Righteousness
That Your Son Needs to Hear from You:

_____

_____

_____

_____

_____

_____

_____

_____

_____

_____

_____

_____

_____

_____

A TIME TO PRAY:
Write Down Your Prayer for Your Son about This Chapter:

Dear Lord,

_____

_____

_____

_____

_____

_____

_____

_____

_____

_____

_____

_____

_____

Amen

SINCE PRIDE USUALLY PRECEDES A FALL, STAY HUMBLE.

*Humble yourselves therefore under
the mighty hand of God,
so that He may exalt you in due time,
casting all your care upon Him,
because He cares about you.*

1 Peter 5:6-7 Holman CSB

TALK TO YOUR SON ABOUT HUMILITY

God's Word clearly instructs us to be humble. And that's good because, as fallible human beings, we have so very much to be humble about. Besides, God promises to bless the humble and correct the prideful. So why, then, are we humans so full of ourselves? The answer, of course, is that, if we are honest with ourselves and with our God, we simply can't be boastful; we should, instead, be eternally grateful and exceedingly humble. Yet humility is not, in most cases, a naturally occurring human trait.

Most of us, grownups and kids alike, are more than willing to overestimate our own accomplishments. We are tempted to say, "Look how wonderful I am!" . . . hoping all the while that the world will agree with our own self-appraisals. But those of us who fall prey to the sin of pride should beware—God is definitely not impressed by our prideful proclamations.

God honors humility . . . and He rewards those who humbly serve Him. So if you've acquired the wisdom to be humble, and if you're teaching your son to do likewise, you are to be congratulated. But if you've not yet overcome the tendency to overestimate your own accomplishments, or if your son seems overly impressed with his own accomplishments, then God still has some important (and perhaps painful) lessons to teach you—lessons about humility that you and your loved ones may still need to learn.

———•◦•———

Clothe yourselves with humility toward one another,
because God resists the proud, but gives grace to the humble.
1 Peter 5:5 Holman CSB

But He said to me, "My grace is sufficient for you,
for power is perfected in weakness." Therefore,
I will most gladly boast all the more about my weaknesses,
so that Christ's power may reside in me.
2 Corinthians 12:9 Holman CSB

You will save the humble people;
But Your eyes are on the haughty,
that You may bring them down.
2 Samuel 22:28 NKJV

MORE FROM GOD'S WORD ABOUT GIVING GOD THE PRAISE HE DESERVES

Praise the Lord, all nations! Glorify Him, all peoples! For great is His faithful love to us; the Lord's faithfulness endures forever. Hallelujah!

Psalm 117 Holman CSB

But I will hope continually and will praise You more and more.

Psalm 71:14 Holman CSB

Therefore, through Him let us continually offer up to God a sacrifice of praise, that is, the fruit of our lips that confess His name.

Hebrews 13:15 Holman CSB

So that at the name of Jesus every knee should bow—of those who are in heaven and on earth and under the earth—and every tongue should confess that Jesus Christ is Lord, to the glory of God the Father.

Philippians 2:10-11 Holman CSB

MORE GREAT IDEAS

I can usually sense that a leading is from the Holy Spirit when it calls me to humble myself, to serve somebody, to encourage somebody, or to give something away. Very rarely will the evil one lead us to do those kind of things.

Bill Hybels

Faith itself cannot be strong where humility is weak.

C. H. Spurgeon

All kindness and good deeds, we must keep silent. The result will be an inner reservoir of personality power.

Catherine Marshall

Let the love of Christ be believed in and felt in your hearts, and it will humble you.

C. H. Spurgeon

We are never stronger than the moment we admit we are weak.

Beth Moore

Because Christ Jesus came to the world clothed in humility, he will always be found among those who are clothed with humility. He will be found among the humble people.

A. W. Tozer

One never can see, or not till long afterwards, why any one was selected for any job. And when one does, it is usually some reason that leaves no room for vanity.

C. S. Lewis

That some of my hymns have been dictated by the blessed Holy Spirit I have no doubt; and that others have been the result of deep meditation I know to be true; but that the poet has any right to claim special merit for himself is certainly presumptuous.

Fanny Crosby

Jesus had a humble heart. If He abides in us, pride will never dominate our lives.

Billy Graham

POINTS OF EMPHASIS:
Write Down at Least Three Things About Humility That
Your Son Needs to Hear from You:

_____

_____

_____

_____

_____

_____

_____

_____

_____

_____

_____

_____

_____

_____

A TIME TO PRAY:
Write Down Your Prayer for Your Son about This Chapter:

Dear Lord,

_____

_____

_____

_____

_____

_____

_____

_____

_____

_____

_____

_____

_____

Amen

IF YOU DON'T CELEBRATE LIFE, NOBODY'S GOING TO CELEBRATE IT FOR YOU.

*This is the day the Lord has made;
let us rejoice and be glad in it.*

–

Psalm 118:24 Holman CSB

TALK TO YOUR SON ABOUT CELEBRATING LIFE THE RIGHT WAY

The 118th Psalm reminds us that today, like every other day, is a cause for celebration. God gives us this day; He fills it to the brim with possibilities, and He challenges us to use it for His purposes. The day is presented to us fresh and clean at midnight, free of charge, but we must beware: Today is a non-renewable resource—once it's gone, it's gone forever. Our responsibility, of course, is to use this day in the service of God's will and according to His commandments.

If your son is like most people, he may, at times, fall victim to the negativity and cynicism of our negative age. And if that happens, it's up to you to remind him that every day is a gift and that he should treasure the time that God has given him.

The Christian life should be a triumphal celebration, a daily exercise in thanksgiving and praise. Encourage your son to join that celebration. And while you're at it, make sure that you've joined in the celebration, too.

Rejoice in the Lord always. I will say it again: Rejoice!
Philippians 4:4 Holman CSB

These things I have spoken to you,
that My joy may remain in you,
and that your joy may be full.

—

John 15:11 NKJV

MORE FROM GOD'S WORD ABOUT CHEERFULNESS

Be cheerful. Keep things in good repair. Keep your spirits up. Think in harmony. Be agreeable. Do all that, and the God of love and peace will be with you for sure.

2 Corinthians 13:11 MSG

Jacob said, "For what a relief it is to see your friendly smile. It is like seeing the smile of God!"

Genesis 33:10 NLT

Do everything readily and cheerfully—no bickering, no second-guessing allowed! Go out into the world uncorrupted, a breath of fresh air in this squalid and polluted society. Provide people with a glimpse of good living and of the living God. Carry the light-giving Message into the night.

Philippians 2:14-15 MSG

Each person should do as he has decided in his heart—not out of regret or out of necessity, for God loves a cheerful giver.

2 Corinthians 9:7 Holman CSB

Their sorrow was turned into rejoicing and their mourning into a holiday. They were to be days of feasting, rejoicing, and of sending gifts to one another and the poor.

Esther 9:22 Holman CSB

MORE GREAT IDEAS

Joy is the direct result of having God's perspective on our daily lives and the effect of loving our Lord enough to obey His commands and trust His promises.

Bill Bright

Our sense of joy, satisfaction, and fulfillment in life increases, no matter what the circumstances, if we are in the center of God's will.

Billy Graham

A life of intimacy with God is characterized by joy.

Oswald Chambers

When we get rid of inner conflicts and wrong attitudes toward life, we will almost automatically burst into joy.

E. Stanley Jones

In the absence of all other joys, the joy of the Lord can fill the soul to the brim.

C. H. Spurgeon

God knows everything. He can manage everything, and He loves us. Surely this is enough for a fullness of joy that is beyond words.

Hannah Whitall Smith

Joy is the serious business
of heaven.

—

C. S. Lewis

Some of us seem so anxious
about avoiding hell that
we forget to celebrate our journey
toward heaven.

—

Philip Yancey

POINTS OF EMPHASIS:
Write Down at Least Three Things About Celebration
That Your Son Needs to Hear from You:

_____

_____

_____

_____

_____

_____

_____

_____

_____

_____

_____

_____

_____

_____

A Time to Pray:
Write Down Your Prayer for Your Son about This Chapter:

Dear Lord,

_____

_____

_____

_____

_____

_____

_____

_____

_____

_____

_____

_____

_____

Amen

OPTIMISM PAYS, PESSIMISM DOESN'T.

But if we hope for what we do not see,
we eagerly wait for it with patience.

—

Romans 8:25 Holman CSB

Talk to Your Son About Optimism

Are you an optimistic, hopeful, enthusiastic Christian? You should be. After all, as a believer, you have every reason to be optimistic about life here on earth and life eternal. As English clergyman William Ralph Inge observed, "No Christian should be a pessimist, for Christianity is a system of radical optimism." Inge's words are most certainly true, but sometimes, you and your loved ones may find yourselves pulled down by the inevitable demands and worries of life here on earth. If so, it's time to ask yourself this question: what's bothering you, and why?

If you're worried by the inevitable challenges of everyday living, God wants to have a little talk with you. After all, the ultimate battle has already been won on the cross at Calvary. And if your life has been transformed by Christ's sacrifice, then you, as a recipient of God's grace, have every reason to live courageously.

Are you willing to trust God's plans for your life, and will you encourage your son to do the same? Hopefully so because even when the challenges of the day seem daunting, God remains steadfast. And, so should you.

So make this promise to yourself and keep it—vow to be a hope-filled parent. Think optimistically about your life, your profession, your family, your future, and your purpose for living. Trust your hopes, not your fears. Take time to celebrate God's glorious creation. And then, when you've filled your heart with hope and gladness, share your optimism with every member of your family. They'll be better for it, and so will you.

Make me hear joy and gladness.
Psalm 51:8 NKJV

For God has not given us a spirit of fearfulness,
but one of power, love, and sound judgment.
2 Timothy 1:7 Holman CSB

Lord, I turn my hope to You.
My God, I trust in You.
Psalm 25:1-2 Holman CSB

Lord, I turn my hope to You.
My God, I trust in You.

—

Psalm 25:1-2 Holman CSB

MORE GREAT IDEAS

It is a remarkable thing that some of the most optimistic and enthusiastic people you will meet are those who have been through intense suffering.

Warren Wiersbe

The Christian lifestyle is not one of legalistic do's and don'ts, but one that is positive, attractive, and joyful.

Vonette Bright

The popular idea of faith is of a certain obstinate optimism: the hope, tenaciously held in the face of trouble, that the universe is fundamentally friendly and things may get better.

J. I. Packer

The people whom I have seen succeed best in life have always been cheerful and hopeful people who went about their business with a smile on their faces.

Charles Kingsley

Developing a positive attitude means working continually to find what is uplifting and encouraging.

Barbara Johnson

Keep your feet on the ground,
but let your heart soar as high as it will.
Refuse to be average or to surrender
to the chill of your spiritual environment.

—

A. W. Tozer

TALKING TO YOUR SON ABOUT HOPE

The hope that the world offers is fleeting and imperfect. The hope that God offers is unchanging, unshakable, and unending. It is no wonder, then, that when we seek security from worldly sources, our hopes are often dashed. Thankfully, God has no such record of failure.

Because we are saved by a risen Christ, we can have hope for the future, no matter how troublesome our present circumstances may seem. After all, God has promised that we are His throughout eternity. And, He has told us that we must place our hopes in Him.

All of us, parents and children alike, will face disappointments and failures while we are here on earth, but these are only temporary defeats. Of course, this world can be a place of trials and tribulations, but when we place our trust in the Giver of all things good, we are secure. God has promised us peace, joy, and eternal life. And God keeps His promises today, tomorrow, and forever.

Are you willing to place your future in the hands of a loving and all-knowing God? Will you face today's challenges with optimism and hope? And will you encourage your son to do the same? Hopefully, you can answer these questions with a resounding yes. After all, God created you and your child for very important purposes: His purposes. And you both still have important work to do: His work.

So today, as you live in the present and look to the future, remember that God has a plan for you and your son. And it's up to both of you to act—and to believe—accordingly.

—◆—

Now may the God of hope fill you with all joy and peace in believing, so that you may overflow with hope by the power of the Holy Spirit.

—

Romans 15:13 Holman CSB

MORE GREAT IDEAS

I wish I could make it all new again; I can't. But God can. "He restores my soul," wrote the shepherd. God doesn't reform; he restores. He doesn't camouflage the old; he restores the new. The Master Builder will pull out the original plan and restore it. He will restore the vigor, he will restore the energy. He will restore the hope. He will restore the soul.

Max Lucado

Faith looks back and draws courage; hope looks ahead and keeps desire alive.

John Eldredge

Hope is nothing more than the expectation of those things which faith has believed to be truly promised by God.

John Calvin

Oh, remember this: There is never a time when we may not hope in God. Whatever our necessities, however great our difficulties, and though to all appearance help is impossible, yet our business is to hope in God, and it will be found that it is not in vain.

George Mueller

The hope we have in Jesus is the anchor for the soul—something sure and steadfast, preventing drifting or giving way, lowered to the depth of God's love.

Franklin Graham

The Christian believes in a fabulous future.

Billy Graham

Take courage. We walk in the wilderness today and in the Promised Land tomorrow.

D. L. Moody

It may be that the day of judgment will dawn tomorrow; in that case, we shall gladly stop working for a better tomorrow. But not before.

Dietrich Bonhoeffer

Joy comes from knowing God loves me and knows who I am and where I'm going . . . that my future is secure as I rest in Him.

James Dobson

POINTS OF EMPHASIS:
Write Down at Least Three Things About Optimism That
Your Son Needs to Hear from You:

_____

_____

_____

_____

_____

_____

_____

_____

_____

_____

_____

_____

_____

_____

A Time to Pray:
Write Down Your Prayer for Your Son about This Chapter:

Dear Lord,

_____

_____

_____

_____

_____

_____

_____

_____

_____

_____

_____

_____

_____

Amen

IT PAYS TO BE RESPECTFUL, SO TREAT EVERYBODY LIKE YOU'D WANT TO BE TREATED IF YOU WERE IN THEIR SHOES.

*Therefore, whatever you want others to do for you,
do also the same for them—
this is the Law and the Prophets.*

–

Matthew 7:12 Holman CSB

Talk to Your Son About Kindness

All over the world, loving parents preach the same lesson: kindness. And Christ taught that very same lesson when He spoke the words recorded in Matthew 7:12.

The Bible instructs us to be courteous and compassionate—and God's Word promises that when we follow these instructions, we are blessed. But sometimes, we fall short. Sometimes, amid the busyness and confusion of everyday life, we may neglect to share a kind word or a kind deed. This oversight hurts others, and it hurts us as well.

The Golden Rule commands us to treat others as we wish to be treated. When we weave the thread of kindness into the very fabric of our lives, we give glory to the One who gave His life for us.

Your son is growing up in a cynical society that often seems to focus on self-gratification and self-centeredness. Yet God's Word warns against becoming too attached to the world, and it's a warning that applies both to your son and to you.

So today, slow yourself down and be alert for those who need a smile, a kind word, or a helping hand. And encourage your son to do the same—encourage him to make kindness a centerpiece of his dealings with others. When he does, he'll discover that life is simply better when he treats other people in the same way he would want to be treated if he were in their shoes.

---

*Finally, all of you be of one mind, having compassion
for one another; love as brothers,
be tenderhearted, be courteous.*
1 Peter 3:8 NKJV

Love is patient; love is kind.
1 Corinthians 13:4 Holman CSB

*And be kind and compassionate to one another,
forgiving one another,
just as God also forgave you in Christ.*
Ephesians 4:32 Holman CSB

More from God's Word About Generosity

So let each one give as he purposes in his heart, not grudgingly or of necessity; for God loves a cheerful giver.

2 Corinthians 9:7 NKJV

Dear friend, you are showing your faith by whatever you do for the brothers, and this you are doing for strangers.

3 John 1:5 Holman CSB

In every way I've shown you that by laboring like this, it is necessary to help the weak and to keep in mind the words of the Lord Jesus, for He said, "It is more blessed to give than to receive."

Acts 20:35 Holman CSB

If a brother or sister is without clothes and lacks daily food, and one of you says to them, "Go in peace, keep warm, and eat well," but you don't give them what the body needs, what good is it?

James 2:15-16 Holman CSB

MORE GREAT IDEAS

The golden rule to follow to obtain spiritual understanding is not one of intellectual pursuit, but one of obedience.

Oswald Chambers

Love is not grabbing, or self-centered, or selfish. Real love is being able to contribute to the happiness of another person without expecting to get anything in return.

James Dobson

Faith never asks whether good works are to be done, but has done them before there is time to ask the question, and it is always doing them.

Martin Luther

We must mirror God's love in the midst of a world full of hatred. We are the mirrors of God's love, so we may show Jesus by our lives.

Corrie ten Boom

When you extend hospitality to others, you're not trying to impress people, you're trying to reflect God to them.

Max Lucado

Be so preoccupied with
good will that you haven't room
for ill will.

—

E. Stanley Jones

IT'S IMPORTANT TO SERVE

If you and your family members genuinely seek to discover God's unfolding priorities for your lives, you must ask yourselves this question: "How does God want us to serve others?" And you may be certain of this: service to others is an integral part of God's plan for your lives, a plan that the Creator intends for you to impart to your son.

Christ was the ultimate servant, the Savior who gave His life for mankind. As His followers, we, too, must become humble servants. As Christians, we are clearly (and repeatedly) instructed to assist those in need. But, as weak human beings, we sometimes fall short as we seek to puff ourselves up and glorify our own accomplishments. Jesus commands otherwise. He teaches us that the most esteemed men and women are not the self-congratulatory leaders of society but are instead the humblest of servants.

Is your family willing to roll up its sleeves and become humble servants for Christ? Are you willing to do your part to make the world a better place? Are you willing to serve God now and trust Him to bless you later? The answer to these questions will determine the direction of your lives and the quality of your service.

As members of God's family, we must serve our neighbors quietly and without fanfare. We must find needs and meet them. We must lend helping hands and share kind words with humility in our hearts and praise on our lips. And we must remember that every time we help someone in need, we are serving our Savior . . . which, by the way, is precisely what we must do.

———————

If they serve Him obediently, they will end their days in prosperity and their years in happiness.
Job 36:11 Holman CSB

We must do the works of Him who sent Me while it is day. Night is coming when no one can work.
John 9:4 Holman CSB

Serve the Lord with gladness.
Psalm 100:2 Holman CSB

More Great Ideas

Before the judgment seat of Christ, my service will not be judged by how much I have done but by how much of me there is in it.

A. W. Tozer

When you're enjoying the fulfillment and fellowship that inevitably accompanies authentic service, ministry is a joy. Instead of exhausting you, it energizes you; instead of burnout, you experience blessing.

Bill Hybels

Make it a rule, and pray to God to help you to keep it, never, if possible, to lie down at night without being able to say: "I have made one human being at least a little wiser, or a little happier, or at least a little better this day."

Charles Kingsley

Opportunities for service abound, and you will be surprised that when you seek God's direction, a place of suitable service will emerge where you can express your love through service.

Charles Stanley

No life can surpass that of a man who quietly continues to serve God in the place where providence has placed him.

—

C. H. Spurgeon

POINTS OF EMPHASIS:
Write Down at Least Three Things About the Golden Rule and Respect That Your Son Needs to Hear from You:

_____

_____

_____

_____

_____

_____

_____

_____

_____

_____

_____

_____

_____

_____

A TIME TO PRAY:
Write Down Your Prayer for Your Son about This Chapter:

Dear Lord,

_____

_____

_____

_____

_____

_____

_____

_____

_____

_____

_____

_____

_____

Amen

YOU'RE NEVER TOO OLD (OR TOO YOUNG) TO LEARN SOMETHING NEW.

*Apply yourself to instruction
and listen to words of knowledge.*

–

Proverbs 23:12 Holman CSB

TALK TO YOUR SON ABOUT
LIFETIME LEARNING

As long as we live, we should continue to learn, and we should encourage our children to do likewise. But sometimes the job of teaching our kids seems to be a thankless one. Why? Because sometimes our children pay scant attention to the educational opportunities that we adults work so hard to provide for them.

Education is the tool by which all of us—parents and children alike—come to know and appreciate the world in which we live. It is the shining light that snuffs out the darkness of ignorance and poverty. Education is freedom just as surely as ignorance is a form of bondage. Education is not a luxury, it is a necessity and a powerful tool for good in this world.

When it comes to learning life's most important lessons, we can either do things the easy way or the hard way. The easy way can be summed up as follows: when God teaches us a lesson, we learn it . . . the first time. Unfortunately, too many of us learn much more slowly than that.

When we resist God's instruction, He continues to teach, whether we like it or not. Our challenge, then, is to discern God's lessons from the experiences of everyday life. Hopefully, we learn those lessons sooner rather than later because the sooner we do, the sooner He can move on to the next lesson and the next, and the next.

So your challenge, as a thoughtful parent, is straight-forward: to convince your son that he still has much to learn, even if your boy would prefer to believe otherwise.

An ear that listens to life-giving rebukes
will be at home among the wise.
Proverbs 15:31 Holman CSB

A wise heart accepts commands,
but foolish lips will be destroyed.
Proverbs 10:8 Holman CSB

He answered them,
"To know the secrets of the kingdom of heaven
has been granted to you . . ."
Matthew 13:12 Holman CSB

More from God's Word About Maturity

But grow in grace, and in the knowledge of our Lord and Saviour Jesus Christ . . . .

2 Peter 3:18 KJV

Consider it a great joy, my brothers, whenever you experience various trials, knowing that the testing of your faith produces endurance. But endurance must do its complete work, so that you may be mature and complete, lacking nothing.

James 1:2-4 Holman CSB

Brothers, I do not consider myself to have taken hold of it. But one thing I do: forgetting what is behind and reaching forward to what is ahead, I pursue as my goal the prize promised by God's heavenly call in Christ Jesus.

Philippians 3:13-14 Holman CSB

You must follow the Lord your God and fear Him. You must keep His commands and listen to His voice; you must worship Him and remain faithful to Him.

Deuteronomy 13:4 Holman CSB

MORE GREAT IDEAS

The wonderful thing about God's schoolroom is that we get to grade our own papers. You see, He doesn't test us so He can learn how well we're doing. He tests us so we can discover how well we're doing.

Charles Swindoll

True learning can take place at every age of life, and it doesn't have to be in the curriculum plan.

Suzanne Dale Ezell

I hope you don't mind me telling you all this. One can learn only by seeing one's mistakes.

C. S. Lewis

The wise man gives proper appreciation in his life to his past. He learns to sift the sawdust of heritage in order to find the nuggets that make the current moment have any meaning.

Grady Nutt

Our loving God uses difficulty in our lives to burn away the sin of self and build faith and spiritual power.

Bill Bright

It's the things you learn
after you know it all
that really count.

—

Vance Havner

TELL YOUR SON:
LIFE IS SHORTER THAN YOU THINK,
SO MAKE EVERY DAY COUNT.

So teach us to number our days, that we may gain a heart of wisdom.

Psalm 90:12 NKJV

Time is a nonrenewable gift from God. But sometimes, all of us—both parents and children alike—treat our time here on earth as if it were not a gift at all: We may be tempted to invest our lives in trivial pursuits and petty diversions. Instead of dong what needs to be done now, we procrastinate. Yet our Father beckons each of us to a higher calling.

If you intend to be a responsible parent, you must teach your son to use time responsibly. After all, each waking moment holds the potential to do a good deed, to say a kind word, to fulfill a personal responsibility, or to offer a heartfelt prayer.

Time is a perishable commodity: we must use it or lose it. So your child's challenge (and yours) is to use the gift of time wisely. To do any less is an affront to the Creator and a prescription for disappointment.

More from God's Word

Therefore, get your minds ready for action, being self-disciplined, and set your hope completely on the grace to be brought to you at the revelation of Jesus Christ.

1 Peter 1:13 Holman CSB

When you make a vow to God, don't delay fulfilling it, because He does not delight in fools. Fulfill what you vow.

Ecclesiastes 5:4 Holman CSB

If you do nothing in a difficult time, your strength is limited.

Proverbs 24:10 Holman CSB

Working together with Him, we also appeal to you: "Don't receive God's grace in vain." For He says: In an acceptable time, I heard you, and in the day of salvation, I helped you. Look, now is the acceptable time; look, now is the day of salvation.

2 Corinthians 6:1-2 Holman CSB

MORE GREAT IDEAS

The more time you give to something, the more you reveal its importance and value to you.

Rick Warren

Our leisure, even our play, is a matter of serious concern. There is no neutral ground in the universe: every square inch, every split second, is claimed by God and counterclaimed by Satan.

C. S. Lewis

The work of God is appointed. There is always enough time to do the will of God.

Elisabeth Elliot

Our time is short! The time we can invest for God, in creative things, in receiving our fellowmen for Christ, is short!

Billy Graham

As we surrender the use of our time to the lordship of Christ, He will lead us to use it in the most productive way imaginable.

Charles Stanley

Stay busy. Get proper exercise.
Eat the right foods.
Don't spend time watching TV,
lying in bed, or napping all day.

—

Truett Cathy

POINTS OF EMPHASIS:
Write Down at Least Three Things About Lifetime Learning That Your Son Needs to Hear from You:

_____

_____

_____

_____

_____

_____

_____

_____

_____

_____

_____

_____

_____

_____

A TIME TO PRAY:
Write Down Your Prayer for Your Son about This Chapter:

Dear Lord,

_____

_____

_____

_____

_____

_____

_____

_____

_____

_____

_____

_____

_____

_____

Amen

DON'T DEPEND ON LUCK, AND WHILE YOU'RE AT IT, DON'T TRY TO GET SOMETHING FOR NOTHING.

Don't be deceived: God is not mocked.
For whatever a man sows he will also reap,
because the one who sows to his flesh will reap
corruption from the flesh,
but the one who sows to the Spirit will reap
eternal life from the Spirit.

–

Galatians 6:7-8 Holman CSB

Talk to Your Son About Responsibility

How hard is it for young people to act responsibly? Sometimes, when youngsters are beset by negative role models and relenting peer pressure, it can be very difficult for them to do the right thing. Difficult, but not impossible.

Nobody needs to tell your son the obvious: He has many responsibilities—obligations to himself, to his family, to his community, to his school, and to his Creator. And which of these duties should take priority? The answer can be found in Matthew 6:33: "But seek first the kingdom of God and His righteousness, and all these things will be provided for you" (Holman CSB).

When your son "seeks first the kingdom of God," all the other obligations have a way of falling into place. And when your son learns the importance of honoring God with his time, his talents, and his prayers, he'll be much more likely to behave responsibly.

So do your youngster a favor: encourage him to take all his duties seriously, especially his duties to God. If he follows your advice, your child will soon discover that pleasing his Father in heaven isn't just the right thing to do; it's also the best way to live.

*But each person should examine his own work,
and then he will have a reason for boasting
in himself alone, and not in respect to someone else.
For each person will have to carry his own load.*

—

Galatians 6:4-5 Holman CSB

More from God's Word About Doing What's Right

Don't be deceived: God is not mocked. For whatever a man sows he will also reap, because the one who sows to his flesh will reap corruption from the flesh, but the one who sows to the Spirit will reap eternal life from the Spirit.

Galatians 6:7-8 Holman CSB

Lead a tranquil and quiet life in all godliness and dignity.

1 Timothy 2:2 Holman CSB

For this very reason, make every effort to supplement your faith with goodness, goodness with knowledge, knowledge with self-control, self-control with endurance, endurance with godliness.

2 Peter 1:5-6 Holman CSB

Therefore as you have received Christ Jesus the Lord, walk in Him.

Colossians 2:6 Holman CSB

MORE GREAT IDEAS

Do not pray for easy lives. Pray to be stronger men! Do not pray for tasks equal to your powers. Pray for powers equal to your tasks.

Phillips Brooks

Whether we know it or not, whether we agree with it or not, whether we practice it or not, whether we like it or not, we are accountable to one another.

Charles Stanley

God never does anything for a man that the man can do for himself. The Lord is too busy for that. So look after your own business and let the Good Lord look after His.

Sam Jones

Action springs not from thought, but from a readiness for responsibility.

Dietrich Bonhoeffer

Our trustworthiness implies His trustworthiness.

Beth Moore

Living life with a consistent
spiritual walk deeply influences
those we love most.

—

Vonette Bright

TALK TO YOUR SON ABOUT AVOIDING NEEDLESS RISKS

Enthusiasm without knowledge is not good. If you act too quickly, you might make a mistake.

Proverbs 19:2 NCV

Is your son, at times, just a bit too impulsive for his own good? Does he occasionally leap before he looks? Does he react first and think about his reaction second? And, as a result, does he occasionally take risks that he should not take? If so, God wants to have a little chat with him.

God's Word is clear: as believers, we are called to lead lives of discipline, diligence, moderation, and maturity. But the world often tempts us to behave otherwise. Everywhere we turn, or so it seems, we are faced with powerful temptations to behave in undisciplined, ungodly ways.

God's Word instructs us to be disciplined in our thoughts and our actions; God's Word warns us against the dangers of impulsive behavior. God's Word teaches us that "anger" is only one letter away from "danger." And, as believers in a just God who means what He says, your son should act—and react—accordingly.

MORE FROM GOD'S WORD ABOUT
AVOIDING NEEDLESS RISKS

The wise inherit honor, but fools are put to shame!

Proverbs 3:35 NLT

Grow a wise heart—you'll do yourself a favor; keep a clear head—you'll find a good life.

Proverbs 19:8 MSG

The one who walks with the wise will become wise, but a companion of fools will suffer harm.

Proverbs 13:20 Holman CSB

But if any of you needs wisdom, you should ask God for it. He is generous and enjoys giving to all people, so he will give you wisdom.

James 1:5 NCV

Those who are wise will shine as bright as the sky, and those who turn many to righteousness will shine like stars forever.

Daniel 12:3 NLT

MORE GREAT IDEAS

The really committed leave the safety of the harbor, accept the risk of the open seas of faith, and set their compasses for the place of total devotion to God and whatever life adventures He plans for them.

Bill Hybels

There comes a time when we simply have to face the challenges in our lives and stop backing down.

John Eldredge

Risk must be taken because the greatest hazard in life is to risk nothing.

John Maxwell

Beware of cut-and-dried theologies that reduce the ways of God to a manageable formula that keeps life safe. God often does the unexplainable just to keep us on our toes— and also on our knees.

Warren Wiersbe

We live in a world where you can afford to fail and try again.

Dennis Swanberg

POINTS OF EMPHASIS:
Write Down at Least Three Things About Responsibility
That Your Son Needs to Hear from You:

_____

_____

_____

_____

_____

_____

_____

_____

_____

_____

_____

_____

_____

A TIME TO PRAY:
Write Down Your Prayer for Your Son about This Chapter:

Dear Lord,

_____

_____

_____

_____

_____

_____

_____

_____

_____

_____

_____

_____

_____

_____

Amen

IT'S IMPORTANT TO KNOW WHEN NOT TO GIVE UP.

Though a righteous man falls seven times,
he will get up,
but the wicked will stumble into ruin.

–

Proverbs 24:16 Holman CSB

TALK TO YOUR SON ABOUT PERSEVERANCE

As he makes his way through life, your son will undoubtedly experience his fair share of disappointments, detours, false starts, and failures. Whenever he encounters one of life's dead ends, he'll face a test of character. So the question of the day is not if your boy will be tested; it's how he will respond.

The old saying is as true today as it was when it was first spoken: "Life is a marathon, not a sprint." That's why wise travelers select a traveling companion who never tires and never falters. That partner, of course, is God.

The next time your son's courage is tested to the limit, remind him that God is always near and that the Creator offers strength and comfort to those who are wise enough to ask for it. Your son's job, of course, is to ask.

God operates on His own timetable, and sometimes He may answer your child's prayers with silence. But if your son remains steadfast, he may soon be surprised at the creative ways that God finds to help determined believers who possess the wisdom and the courage to persevere.

A patient spirit is better than a proud spirit.
Ecclesiastes 7:8 Holman CSB

*So we must not get tired of doing good,
for we will reap at the proper time
if we don't give up.*

—

Galatians 6:9 Holman CSB

MORE FROM GOD'S WORD ABOUT PATIENCE

And we exhort you, brothers: warn those who are lazy, comfort the discouraged, help the weak, be patient with everyone.

1 Thessalonians 5:14 Holman CSB

I, therefore, the prisoner in the Lord, urge you to walk worthy of the calling you have received, with all humility and gentleness, with patience, accepting one another in love. . . .

Ephesians 4:1-2 Holman CSB

Wherefore seeing we also are compassed about with so great a cloud of witnesses, let us lay aside every weight, and the sin which doth so easily beset us, and let us run with patience the race that is set before us . . . .

Hebrews 12:1 KJV

Therefore the Lord is waiting to show you mercy, and is rising up to show you compassion, for the Lord is a just God. Happy are all who wait patiently for Him.

Isaiah 30:18 Holman CSB

More Great Ideas

Battles are won in the trenches, in the grit and grime of courageous determination; they are won day by day in the arena of life.

Charles Swindoll

You cannot persevere unless there is a trial in your life. There can be no victories without battles; there can be no peaks without valleys. If you want the blessing, you must be prepared to carry the burden and fight the battle. God has to balance privileges with responsibilities, blessings with burdens, or else you and I will become spoiled, pampered children.

Warren Wiersbe

Perseverance is more than endurance. It is endurance combined with absolute assurance and certainty that what we are looking for is going to happen.

Oswald Chambers

Only the man who follows the command of Jesus single-mindedly and unresistingly lets his yoke rest upon him, finds his burden easy, and under its gentle pressure receives the power to persevere in the right way.

Dietrich Bonhoeffer

By perseverance
the snail reached the ark.

—

C. H. Spurgeon

Tell Your Son:
You Can't Win Them All;
Don't Waste Time Regretting
the Ones You Lose.

One thing I do, forgetting those things which are behind and reaching forward to those things which are ahead, I press toward the goal for the prize of the upward call of God in Christ Jesus.

Philippians 3:13-14 NKJV

Do not remember the past events, pay no attention to things of old. Look, I am about to do something new; even now it is coming. Do you not see it? Indeed, I will make a way in the wilderness, rivers in the desert.

Isaiah 43:18-19 Holman CSB

Consider it a great joy, my brothers, whenever you experience various trials, knowing that the testing of your faith produces endurance. But endurance must do its complete work, so that you may be mature and complete, lacking nothing.

James 1:2-4 Holman CSB

I will thank you, Lord, with all my heart; I will tell of all the marvelous things you have done. I will be filled with joy because of you. I will sing praises to your name, O Most High.

Psalm 9:1-2 NLT

More Great Ideas

Get rid of the poison of built-up anger and the acid of long-term resentment

Charles Swindoll

Leave the broken, irreversible past in God's hands, and step out into the invincible future with Him.

Oswald Chambers

In the Christian story God descends to reascend. He comes down; . . . down to the very roots and sea-bed of the Nature he has created. But He goes down to come up again and bring the whole ruined world with Him.

C. S. Lewis

The enemy of our souls loves to taunt us with past failures, wrongs, disappointments, disasters, and calamities. And if we let him continue doing this, our life becomes a long and dark tunnel, with very little light at the end.

Charles Swindoll

He is ever faithful and gives us the song in the night to soothe our spirits and fresh joy each morning to lift our souls. What a marvelous Lord!

Bill Bright

There is no road back
to yesterday.

—

Oswald Chambers

POINTS OF EMPHASIS:
Write Down at Least Three Things About Perseverance
That Your Son Needs to Hear from You:

_____

_____

_____

_____

_____

_____

_____

_____

_____

_____

_____

_____

_____

A TIME TO PRAY:
Write Down Your Prayer for Your Son about This Chapter:

Dear Lord,

_____

_____

_____

_____

_____

_____

_____

_____

_____

_____

_____

_____

_____

_____

_____

Amen

YOU CAN CONTROL THE DIRECTION OF YOUR THOUGHTS, AND YOU SHOULD.

Finally brothers, whatever is true, whatever is honorable, whatever is just, whatever is pure, whatever is lovely, whatever is commendable— if there is any moral excellence and if there is any praise—dwell on these things.

Philippians 4:8 Holman CSB

Talk to Your Son About Thinking Positive Thoughts

Do you pay careful attention to the quality of your thoughts? And are you teaching your son to do likewise? Hopefully so, because the quality of your thoughts will help determine the quality of your lives.

Ours is a society that focuses on—and often glamorizes—the negative aspects of life. So both you and your son will be bombarded with messages—some subtle and some overt—that encourage you to think cynically about your circumstances, your world, and your faith. But God has other plans for you and your youngster.

God promises those who follow His Son can experience joyful abundance (John 10:10). Consequently, Christianity and pessimism simply don't mix. So if you find that your thoughts are being hijacked by the negativity that seems to have invaded our troubled world, it's time to focus less on your challenges and more on God's blessings.

God intends for you and your family members to experience joy and abundance, not cynicism and negativity. So, today and every day hereafter, celebrate the life that God has given you by focusing your thoughts upon those things that are worthy of praise. And while you're at it, teach your son to do the same. When you do, you'll both discover that God's gifts are simply too glorious, and too numerous, to count.

Set your minds on what is above,
not on what is on the earth.
Colossians 3:2 Holman CSB

Commit your works to the Lord,
and your thoughts will be established.
Proverbs 16:3 NKJV

Brothers, don't be childish in your thinking,
but be infants in evil and adult in your thinking.
1 Corinthians 14:20 Holman CSB

Guard your heart above all else,
for it is the source of life.

—

Proverbs 4:23 Holman CSB

MORE FROM GOD'S WORD ABOUT GOD'S BLESSINGS

You will show me the path of life; in Your presence is fullness of joy; at Your right hand are pleasures forevermore.

Psalm 16:11 NKJV

I will make them and the area around My hill a blessing: I will send down showers in their season—showers of blessing.

Ezekiel 34:26 Holman CSB

Obey My voice, and I will be your God, and you shall be my people. And walk in all the ways that I have commanded you, that it may be well with you.

Jeremiah 7:23 NKJV

The Lord bless you and keep you; the Lord make His face shine upon you, and be gracious to you.

Numbers 6:24-25 NKJV

Blessed is a man who endures trials, because when he passes the test he will receive the crown of life that He has promised to those who love Him.

James 1:12 Holman CSB

MORE GREAT IDEAS

Preoccupy my thoughts with your praise beginning today.

Joni Eareckson Tada

Every major spiritual battle is in the mind.

Charles Stanley

Attitude is the mind's paintbrush; it can color any situation.

Barbara Johnson

Your thoughts are the determining factor as to whose mold you are conformed to. Control your thoughts and you control the direction of your life.

Charles Stanley

Beware of cut-and-dried theologies that reduce the ways of God to a manageable formula that keeps life safe. God often does the unexplainable just to keep us on our toes— and also on our knees.

Warren Wiersbe

I became aware of one very important concept I had missed before: my attitude—not my circumstances—was what was making me unhappy.

Vonette Bright

POINTS OF EMPHASIS:

Write Down at Least Three Things About Having Positive Thoughts and a Good Attitude That Your Son Needs to Hear from You:

_____

_____

_____

_____

_____

_____

_____

_____

_____

_____

_____

_____

_____

_____

_____

A TIME TO PRAY:
Write Down Your Prayer for Your Son about This Chapter:

Dear Lord,

_____

_____

_____

_____

_____

_____

_____

_____

_____

_____

_____

_____

Amen

SINCE YOU'LL INEVITABLY BECOME MORE LIKE YOUR FRIENDS, CHOOSE YOUR FRIENDS WISELY.

Do not be deceived:
"Bad company corrupts good morals."

–

1 Corinthians 15:33 Holman CSB

Talk to Your Son About Peer Pressure

Peer pressure can be a good thing or a bad thing for your son, depending upon his peers. If his peers encourage him to make integrity a habit—if they encourage him to follow God's will and to obey God's commandments—your son will experience positive peer pressure, and that's good.

But, if your youngster becomes involved with people who encourage him to do foolish things, he'll face a different kind of peer pressure. If your son feels pressured to do things or to say things that lead him away from God, he's aiming straight for trouble.

As you talk to your child about the differences between positive and negative peer pressure, here are a few things to emphasize:

1. Peer pressure exists, and your son will experience it.

2. If your son's friends encourage him to honor God and become a better person, peer pressure can be a good thing.

3. If your son's friends encourage him to misbehave or underachieve, that sort of peer pressure is destructive.

4. When peer pressure turns negative, it's up to your son to start finding new friends. Today.

To sum it up, your boy has a choice: he can choose to please God first, or he can fall prey to negative peer pressure. The choice is his—and so are the consequences.

———◆◆———

He who walks with wise men will be wise,
but the companion of fools will be destroyed.
Proverbs 13:20 NKJV

Stay away from a foolish man;
you will gain no knowledge from his speech.
Proverbs 14:7 Holman CSB

My son, if sinners entice you, don't be persuaded.
Proverbs 1:10 Holman CSB

MORE GREAT IDEAS

Comparison is the root of all feelings of inferiority.

James Dobson

You must never sacrifice your relationship with God for the sake of a relationship with another person.

Charles Stanley

It is comfortable to know that we are responsible to God and not to man. It is a small matter to be judged of man's judgement.

Lottie Moon

You should forget about trying to be popular with everybody and start trying to be popular with God Almighty.

Sam Jones

If you choose to awaken a passion for God, you will have to choose your friends wisely.

Lisa Bevere

People who constantly, and fervently, seek the approval of others live with an identity crisis. They don't know who they are, and they are defined by what others think of them.

Charles Stanley

True friends will always
lift you higher and challenge you
to walk in a manner pleasing
to our Lord.

—

Lisa Bevere

TALKING TO YOUR SON ABOUT CHARACTER

I t has been said that character is what we are when nobody is watching. How true. When we do things that we know aren't right, we try to hide them from our families and friends. But even if we successfully conceal our sins from the world, we can never conceal our sins from God.

Charles Swindoll correctly observed, "Nothing speaks louder or more powerfully than a life of integrity." Wise parents agree.

Integrity is built slowly over a lifetime. It is the sum of every right decision and every honest word. It is forged on the anvil of honorable work and polished by the twin virtues of honesty and fairness. Integrity is a precious thing—difficult to build but easy to tear down.

Living a life of integrity isn't always the easiest way, especially for a young person like your son. After all, he inhabits a world that presents him with countless temptations to stray far from God's path. So as a parent, your job is to remind him (again and again) that whenever he's confronted with sin, he should walk—or better yet run—in the opposite direction. And the good news is this: When your son makes up his mind to walk with Jesus every day, his character will take care of itself . . . and he won't need to look over his shoulder to see who, besides God, is watching.

———•◦•———

As the water reflects the face,
so the heart reflects the person.
Proverbs 27:19 Holman CSB

We also rejoice in our afflictions, because we know that
affliction produces endurance, endurance produces proven
character, and proven character produces hope.
Romans 5:3-4 Holman CSB

In all things showing yourself to be a pattern of good works;
in doctrine showing integrity,
reverence, incorruptibility . . . .
Titus 2:7 NKJV

MORE GREAT IDEAS

Integrity is the glue that holds our way of life together. We must constantly strive to keep our integrity intact. When wealth is lost, nothing is lost; when health is lost, something is lost; when character is lost, all is lost.

Billy Graham

Integrity is not a given factor in everyone's life. It is a result of self-discipline, inner trust, and a decision to be relentlessly honest in all situations in our lives.

John Maxwell

Honesty has a beautiful and refreshing simplicity about it. No ulterior motives. No hidden meanings. As honesty and integrity characterize our lives, there will be no need to manipulate others.

Charles Swindoll

The single most important element in any human relationship is honesty—with oneself, with God, and with others.

Catherine Marshall

POINTS OF EMPHASIS:
Write Down at Least Three Things About Peer Pressure
That Your Son Needs to Hear from You:

_____

_____

_____

_____

_____

_____

_____

_____

_____

_____

_____

_____

_____

A TIME TO PRAY:
Write Down Your Prayer for Your Son about This Chapter:

Dear Lord,

_____

_____

_____

_____

_____

_____

_____

_____

_____

_____

_____

_____

_____

Amen

MATERIAL POSSESSIONS AREN'T AS IMPORTANT AS YOU THINK. ONCE YOU HAVE ENOUGH, THE OTHER STUFF DOESN'T REALLY MATTER VERY MUCH.

No one can be a slave of two masters,
since either he will hate one and love the other,
or be devoted to one and despise the other.
You cannot be slaves of
God and of money.

—

Matthew 6:24 Holman CSB

Talk to Your Son About Materialism

Your son inhabits a world in which material possessions are, at times, glamorized and, at other times, almost worshipped. The media often glorifies material possessions above all else, but God most certainly does not. And it's up to you, as a responsible parent, to make certain that your child understands that materialism is a spiritual trap, a trap that should be avoided at all costs.

Martin Luther observed, "Many things I have tried to grasp and have lost. That which I have placed in God's hands I still have." His words apply to all of us. Our earthly riches are transitory; our spiritual riches, on the other hand, are everlasting.

If you find yourself wrapped up in the concerns of the material world, you can be sure that your family members are wrapped up in it, too. So how much stuff is too much stuff? It's a tough question for many of us, yet the answer is straightforward: If our possessions begin to interfere with our desire to know and serve God, then we own too many possessions, period.

On the grand stage of a well-lived life, material possessions should play a rather small role. Of course, we all need the basic necessities of life, but once we meet those needs for ourselves and for our families, the piling up of possessions creates more problems than it solves. Our real riches, of course, are not of this world. We are never really rich until we are rich in spirit.

So, if you or your family members find yourselves wrapped up in the concerns of the material world, it's time to reorder your priorities. And, it's time to begin storing up riches that will endure throughout eternity—the spiritual kind.

———

And He told them, "Watch out and be on guard against all greed, because one's life is not in the abundance of his possessions."
Luke 12:15 Holman CSB

For the mind-set of the flesh is death, but the mind-set of the Spirit is life and peace.
Romans 8:6 Holman CSB

More from God's Word About Worldliness

Let no one deceive himself. If anyone among you seems to be wise in this age, let him become a fool that he may become wise. For the wisdom of this world is foolishness with God. For it is written, "He catches the wise in their own craftiness."

1 Corinthians 3:18-19 NKJV

Do not love the world or the things that belong to the world. If anyone loves the world, love for the Father is not in him.

1 John 2:15 Holman CSB

For whatever is born of God overcomes the world. And this is the victory that has overcome the world—our faith.

1 John 5:4 NKJV

Pure and undefiled religion before our God and Father is this: to look after orphans and widows in their distress and to keep oneself unstained by the world.

James 1:27 Holman CSB

MORE GREAT IDEAS

If you want to be truly happy, you won't find it on an endless quest for more stuff. You'll find it in receiving God's generosity and in passing that generosity along.

Bill Hybels

The Scriptures also reveal warning that if we are consumed with greed, not only do we disobey God, but we will miss the opportunity to allow Him to use us as instruments for others.

Charles Stanley

Here's a simple test: If you can see it, it's not going to last. The things that last are the things you cannot see.

Dennis Swanberg

Why is love of gold more potent than love of souls?

Lottie Moon

The cross is laid on every Christian. It begins with the call to abandon the attachments of this world.

Dietrich Bonhoeffer

We own too many things
that aren't worth owning.

—

Marie T. Freeman

TALKING TO YOUR SON ABOUT MANAGING MONEY

As a parent, you know, from firsthand experience, that the job of raising your son is an immense responsibility. And one of your parental duties is to teach your youngster how to manage money.

If you're serious about helping your son become a savvy spender and a serious saver, you must teach by example. After all, parental pronouncements are far easier to make than they are to live by. Yet your son will likely learn far more from your actions than from your words. So please remember that in matters of money, you are not just a role model; you are the role model. And as you begin to teach your child a few common-sense principles about spending and saving, remember that your actions will speak far more loudly than your words.

The world won't protect your son from the consequences of frivolous spending, and neither should you. So if he overspends, don't be too quick to bail him out of his troubles. As a parent, your job is not necessarily to protect your youngster from pain, but to ensure that he learns from the consequences of his actions.

Thankfully, the basic principles of money management aren't very hard to understand. These principles can be summed up in three simple steps:

1. Have a budget and live by it, spending less than you make;

2. Save and invest wisely;

3. Give God His fair share.

These steps are so straightforward that even a young child can grasp them, so you need not have attended business school (or seminary) to teach powerful lessons about faith and finances. And that's good because your son needs your sound advice and good example . . . but not necessarily in that order.

———◦◦◦———

And my God shall supply all your need according to His riches in glory by Christ Jesus.
Philippians 4:19 NKJV

Commit your activities to the Lord and your plans will be achieved.
Proverbs 16:3 Holman CSB

There is nothing wrong with
asking God's direction.
But it is wrong to go our own way,
then expect Him to bail us out.

———

Larry Burkett

Tell Your Son:
The Sooner You Learn to Manage Money, the Better.
So You Might as Well Learn Now.

Good planning and hard work lead to prosperity, but hasty shortcuts lead to poverty.

Proverbs 21:5 NLT

Here's a recipe for handling money wisely: Take a heaping helping of common sense, add a sizeable portion of self-discipline, and mix with prayer.

Marie T. Freeman

Sadly, family problems and even financial problems are seldom the real problem, but often the symptom of a weak or nonexistent value system.

Dave Ramsey

As faithful stewards of what we have, ought we not to give earnest thought to our staggering surplus?

Elisabeth Elliot

POINTS OF EMPHASIS:
Write Down at Least Three Things About Materialism That Your Son Needs to Hear from You:

_____

_____

_____

_____

_____

_____

_____

_____

_____

_____

_____

_____

_____

_____

A TIME TO PRAY:
Write Down Your Prayer for Your Son about This Chapter:

Dear Lord,

_____

_____

_____

_____

_____

_____

_____

_____

_____

_____

_____

_____

_____

Amen

THE WORLD IS FILLED WITH TEMPTATIONS THAT CAN WRECK YOUR LIFE. BEHAVE ACCORDINGLY.

My son, if sinners entice you,
don't be persuaded.

–

Proverbs 1:10 Holman CSB

Talk to Your Son About Temptation

Because our world is filled with temptations, your son will encounter them at every turn. The devil, it seems, is working overtime these days, causing heartache in more places and in more ways than ever before. So your youngster must remain vigilant. How? By avoiding those places where Satan can most easily tempt him and by arming himself with God's Holy Word.

After fasting forty days and nights in the desert, Jesus Himself was tempted by Satan. Christ used Scripture to rebuke the devil (Matthew 4:1-11). We must do likewise. The Holy Bible provides us with a perfect blueprint for righteous living. If we consult that blueprint each day and follow its instructions carefully, we build our lives according to God's plan. And when we do, we are secure.

Your youngster lives in a society that encourages him to "try" any number of things that are dangerous to his spiritual, mental, or physical health. It's a world brimming with traps and temptations designed to corrupt his character, ruin his health, sabotage his relationships, and derail his future. Your job, as a thoughtful parent, is to warn your son of these dangers . . . and to keep warning him.

Be sober! Be on the alert!
Your adversary the Devil is prowling around
like a roaring lion,
looking for anyone he can devour.

—

1 Peter 5:8 Holman CSB

MORE FROM GOD'S WORD ABOUT GUARDING AGAINST EVIL

Guard your heart above all else, for it is the source of life.

Proverbs 4:23 Holman CSB

The peace of God, which surpasses all understanding, will guard your hearts and minds through Christ Jesus.

Philippians 4:7 NKJV

Do not be conformed to this age, but be transformed by the renewing of your mind, so that you may discern what is the good, pleasing, and perfect will of God.

Romans 12:2 Holman CSB

Therefore, submit to God. But resist the Devil, and he will flee from you. Draw near to God, and He will draw near to you. Cleanse your hands, sinners, and purify your hearts, double-minded people!

James 4:7-8 Holman CSB

MORE GREAT IDEAS

It is easier to stay out of temptation than to get out of it.

Rick Warren

In the worst temptations nothing can help us but faith that God's Son has put on flesh, sits at the right hand of the Father, and prays for us. There is no mightier comfort.

Martin Luther

Most Christians do not know or fully realize that the adversary of our lives is Satan and that his main tool is our flesh, our old nature.

Bill Bright

A man who gives in to temptation after five minutes simply does not know what it would have been like an hour later.

C. S. Lewis

Take a really honest look at yourself. Have any old sins begun to take control again? This would be a wonderful time to allow Him to bring fresh order out of longstanding chaos.

Charles Swindoll

Since you are tempted
without ceasing,
pray without ceasing.

—

C. H. Spurgeon

TALKING TO YOUR SON ABOUT ADDICTION

Your son inhabits a society that glamorizes the use of drugs, alcohol, cigarettes, and other addictive substances. Why? The answer can be summed up in one word: money. Simply put, addictive substances are big money makers, so suppliers (of both legal and illegal substances) work overtime to make certain that youngsters like your son sample their products. Since the suppliers need a steady stream of new customers because the old ones are dying off (fast), they engage in a no-holds-barred struggle to find new users—or more accurately, new abusers.

The dictionary defines addiction as "the compulsive need for a habit-forming substance; the condition of being habitually and compulsively occupied with something." That definition is accurate, but incomplete. For Christians, addiction has an additional meaning: it means compulsively worshipping something other than God.

Your son may already know youngsters who are full-blown addicts, but with God's help he can avoid that fate. To do so, he should learn that addictive substances are, in truth, spiritual and emotional poisons. And he must avoid the temptation to experiment with addictive substances. If he can do these things, he will spare himself a lifetime of headaches and heartaches.

TELL YOUR SON:
ADDICTIONS CAN WRECK YOUR LIFE,
AND THE EASIEST WAY TO QUIT
IS NEVER TO START.

You shall have no other gods before Me.

Exodus 20:3 NKJV

For we do not have a High Priest who cannot sympathize with our weaknesses, but was in all points tempted as we are, yet without sin. Let us therefore come boldly to the throne of grace, that we may obtain mercy and find grace to help in time of need.

Hebrews 4:15-16 NKJV

Jesus responded, "I assure you: Everyone who commits sin is a slave of sin."

John 8:34 Holman CSB

Death is the reward of an undisciplined life; your foolish decisions trap you in a dead end.

Proverbs 5:23 MSG

Yet in all these things we are more than conquerors through Him who loved us.

Romans 8:37 NKJV

MORE GREAT IDEAS ABOUT ABSTINENCE, MODERATION, VIRTUE, AND GOD

Virtue—even attempted virtue—brings light; indulgence brings fog.

C. S. Lewis

To many, total abstinence is easier than perfect moderation.

St. Augustine

God is able to take mistakes, when they are committed to Him, and make of them something for our good and for His glory.

Ruth Bell Graham

When we face an impossible situation, all self-reliance and self-confidence must melt away; we must be totally dependent on Him for the resources.

Anne Graham Lotz

No matter how crazy or nutty your life has seemed, God can make something strong and good out of it. He can help you grow wide branches for others to use as shelter.

Barbara Johnson

A person may not be responsible
for his last drink,
but he certainly was for the first.

Billy Graham

Addiction is the most powerful
psychic enemy of humanity's desire
for God.

Gerald May

POINTS OF EMPHASIS:
Write Down at Least Three Things About Temptation
That Your Son Needs to Hear from You:

_____

_____

_____

_____

_____

_____

_____

_____

_____

_____

_____

_____

_____

_____

_____

A Time to Pray:
Write Down Your Prayer for Your Son about This Chapter:

Dear Lord,

_____

_____

_____

_____

_____

_____

_____

_____

_____

_____

_____

_____

_____

_____

_____

Amen

HARD WORK PAYS TREMENDOUS DIVIDENDS, SO THE TIME TO GET BUSY IS NOW.

*We must do the works of Him
who sent Me while it is day.
Night is coming when no one can work.*

–

John 9:4 Holman CSB

TALK TO YOUR SON ABOUT WORK

Has your son acquired the habit of doing first things first, or is he one of those youngsters who puts off important work until the last minute? The answer to this simple question will help determine how well he does in school, how quickly he succeeds in the workplace, and how much satisfaction he derives along the way.

God's Word teaches the value of hard work. In his second letter to the Thessalonians, Paul warns, ". . . if any would not work, neither should he eat" (3:10 KJV). And the Book of Proverbs proclaims, "One who is slack in his work is brother to one who destroys" (18:9 NIV). In short, God has created a world in which diligence is rewarded and laziness is not. And as a parent, it's up to you to convey this message to your son using both words and example (with a decided emphasis on the latter).

Your son will undoubtedly have countless opportunities to accomplish great things—but he should not expect life's greatest rewards to be delivered on a silver platter. Instead, he should pray as if everything depended upon God, but work as if everything depended upon himself. When he does, he can expect very big payoffs indeed.

*Whatever your hands find to do,
do with [all] your strength.*

—

Ecclesiastes 9:10 Holman CSB

More from God's Word About Success

Success, success to you, and success to those who help you, for your God will help you . . . .

1 Chronicles 12:18 NIV

But as for you, be strong; don't be discouraged, for your work has a reward.

2 Chronicles 15:7 Holman CSB

So we must not get tired of doing good, for we will reap at the proper time if we don't give up.

Galatians 6:9 Holman CSB

You need to persevere so that when you have done the will of God, you will receive what he has promised.

Hebrews 10:36 NIV

The one who understands a matter finds success, and the one who trusts in the Lord will be happy.

Proverbs 16:20 Holman CSB

More Great Ideas

We must trust as if it all depended on God and work as if it all depended on us.

C. H. Spurgeon

It may be that the day of judgment will dawn tomorrow; in that case, we shall gladly stop working for a better tomorrow. But not before.

Dietrich Bonhoeffer

The world does not consider labor a blessing, therefore it flees and hates it, but the pious who fear the Lord labor with a ready and cheerful heart, for they know God's command, and they acknowledge His calling.

Martin Luther

I seem to have been led, little by little, toward my work; and I believe that the same fact will appear in the life of anyone who will cultivate such powers as God has given him and then go on, bravely, quietly, but persistently, doing such work as comes to his hands.

Fanny Crosby

Few things fire up a person's commitment like dedication to excellence.

John Maxwell

Freedom is not an absence of responsibility; but rather a reward we receive when we've performed our responsibility with excellence.

Charles Swindoll

He will clothe you in rags if you clothe yourself with idleness.

C. H. Spurgeon

If, in your working hours, you make the work your end, you will presently find yourself all unawares inside the only circle in your profession that really matters. You will be one of the sound craftsmen, and other sound craftsmen will know it.

C. S. Lewis

Thank God every morning when you get up that you have something which must be done, whether you like it or not. Work breeds a hundred virtues that idleness never knows.

Charles Kingsley

OPPORTUNITIES ARE EVERYWHERE, SO KEEP YOUR EYES AND YOUR HEART OPEN.

Therefore, as we have opportunity, we must work for the good of all, especially for those who belong to the household of faith.

Galatians 6:10 Holman CSB

Because we are saved by a risen Christ, we can have hope for the future, no matter how troublesome our present circumstances may seem. After all, God has promised that we are His throughout eternity. And, He has told us that we must place our trust in Him.

Of course, we will face disappointments and failures while we are here on earth, but these are only temporary defeats. Of course, this world can be a place of trials and tribulations, but when we place our trust in the Giver of all things good, we are secure. God has promised us peace, joy, and eternal life. And God keeps His promises.

Whether you realize it or not, opportunities are whirling around you and your family like stars crossing the night sky: beautiful to observe, but too numerous to count. Yet you may be too concerned with the challenges of everyday living to notice those opportunities. That's why you should slow down occasionally, catch your breath, and focus your thoughts on two things: the talents and the opportunities that God has placed before you and your loved ones. God is leading you and your family in the direction of those opportunities. Your task is to watch carefully, to pray fervently, and to act accordingly.

You will show me the path of life; in Your presence is fullness of joy; at Your right hand are pleasures forevermore.

Psalm 16:11 NKJV

For I know the thoughts that I think toward you, says the Lord, thoughts of peace and not of evil, to give you a future and a hope. Then you will call upon Me and go and pray to Me, and I will listen to you.

Jeremiah 29:11-12 NKJV

But Jesus looked at them and said, "With men this is impossible, but with God all things are possible."

Matthew 19:26 Holman CSB

For God has not given us a spirit of fearfulness, but one of power, love, and sound judgment.

2 Timothy 1:7 Holman CSB

I am able to do all things through Him who strengthens me.

Philippians 4:13 Holman CSB

MORE GREAT IDEAS

Life is a glorious opportunity.

Billy Graham

We are all faced with a series of great opportunities, brilliantly disguised as unsolvable problems. Unsolvable without God's wisdom, that is.

Charles Swindoll

God has given you a unique set of talents and opportunities—talents and opportunities that can be built up or buried—and the choice to build or bury is entirely up to you.

Criswell Freeman

A wise man makes more opportunities than he finds.

Francis Bacon

With the right attitude and a willingness to pay the price, almost anyone can pursue nearly any opportunity and achieve it.

John Maxwell

He who waits until circumstances completely favor his undertaking will never accomplish anything.

Martin Luther

Great opportunities
often disguise themselves
in small tasks.

—

Rick Warren

POINTS OF EMPHASIS:
Write Down at Least Three Things About Work That
Your Son Needs to Hear from You:

_____

_____

_____

_____

_____

_____

_____

_____

_____

_____

_____

_____

_____

_____

_____

A TIME TO PRAY:
Write Down Your Prayer for Your Son about This Chapter:

Dear Lord,

_____

_____

_____

_____

_____

_____

_____

_____

_____

_____

_____

_____

_____

Amen

AS YOU GROW OLDER, THINGS WILL HAPPEN THAT YOU SIMPLY CANNOT UNDERSTAND UNLESS YOU REMEMBER THAT GOD HAS AN ETERNAL PERSPECTIVE.

Set your minds on what is above,
not on what is on the earth.

–

Colossians 3:2 Holman CSB

Talk to Your Son About Maintaining Proper Perspective

For parents and kids alike, life is busy and complicated. Amid the rush and crush of the daily grind, it is easy to lose perspective . . . easy, but wrong. When our world seems to be spinning out of control, we can regain perspective by slowing down long enough to put things in proper perspective. But slowing down isn't always easy, especially for young people. So your son may, on occasion, become convinced (wrongly) that today's problems are both permanent and catastrophic. And if he starts making mountains out of molehills, it's up to you, as a thoughtful parent, to teach him how to regain perspective.

When you have a problem that seems overwhelming, do you carve out quiet moments to think about God's promises and what those promises mean in the grand scope of eternity? Are you wise enough to offer thanksgiving and praise to your Creator, in good times and bad? And do you encourage your son to do the same? If so, your child will be blessed by your instruction and your example.

The familiar words of Psalm 46:10 remind us to "Be still, and know that I am God" (NKJV). When we do so, we encounter the awesome presence of our Heavenly Father. But, when we ignore the presence of our Creator, we rob ourselves of His perspective, His peace, and His joy.

So today and every day, make time to be still before the Creator, and encourage your son to do likewise. Then, both of you can face life's inevitable setbacks—all of which, by the way, are temporary setbacks—with the wisdom and power that only God can provide.

———

Now if any of you lacks wisdom, he should ask God,
who gives to all generously and without criticizing,
and it will be given to him.
James 1:5 Holman CSB

I will instruct you and show you the way to go;
with My eye on you, I will give counsel.
Psalm 32:8 Holman CSB

MORE FROM GOD'S WORD ABOUT WISDOM

Don't abandon wisdom, and she will watch over you; love her, and she will guard you.

Proverbs 4:6 Holman CSB

Acquire wisdom—how much better it is than gold! And acquire understanding—it is preferable to silver.

Proverbs 16:16 Holman CSB

The one who acquires good sense loves himself; one who safeguards understanding finds success.

Proverbs 19:8 Holman CSB

Pay careful attention, then, to how you walk—not as unwise people but as wise.

Ephesians 5:15 Holman CSB

Who is wise and understanding among you? Let him show by good conduct that his works are done in the meekness of wisdom.

James 3:13 NKJV

MORE GREAT IDEAS

Life: the time God gives you to determine how you spend eternity.

Anonymous

As you and I lay up for ourselves living, lasting treasures in Heaven, we come to the awesome conclusion that we ourselves are His treasure!

Anne Graham Lotz

Salvation involves so much more than knowing facts about Jesus Christ, or even having special feelings toward Jesus Christ. Salvation comes to us when, by an act of will, we receive Christ as our Savior and Lord.

Warren Wiersbe

We are always trying to "find ourselves" when that is exactly what we need to lose.

Vance Havner

I now know the power of the risen Lord! He lives! The dawn of Easter has broken in my own soul! My night is gone!

Mrs. Charles E. Cowman

Going to church does not make you
a Christian anymore than going to McDonalds
makes you a hamburger.

—

Anonymous

God is God. He knows what he is doing.
When you can't trace his hand,
trust his heart.

—

Max Lucado

TALKING TO YOUR SON ABOUT REGRET

As the old saying goes, "You win some, and you lose some." It's a simple lesson, but probably a tough lesson for your son to learn. After all, your youngster inhabits a society that glorifies winners and minimizes losers. So when your boy wins, he's encouraged—at least by a growing collection of chest-thumping sports icons—to engage in wild, in-your-face celebrations. And when he loses, he's encouraged—at least on a subconscious level—to consider himself "a loser." Yet nothing could be further from the truth. Real success has little to do with the temporary wins and losses of everyday life. Real victory comes when we choose to follow to trust God's Word and follow God's Son.

If your son is bitter about some past defeat, you should remind him that bitterness is a spiritual sickness, a potentially destructive emotion that can rob him of happiness and peace.

So how can your son rid himself of regret? First, he should prayerfully ask God to cleanse his heart. Then, he must learn to catch himself whenever feelings of anger or bitterness to invade his thoughts. In short, he must learn to recognize and to resist negative thoughts before those thoughts hijack his emotions.

The great sports writer Grantland Rice wrote, "For when the one Great Scorer comes to write against your name, He marks not that you won or lost, but how you played the game." That's a message that your son needs to learn now—and if you're a savvy parent, you'll help him learn it. Now.

———◆———

Our yesterdays present irreparable things
to us; it is true that we have lost opportunities
which will never return, but God can
transform this destructive anxiety into
a constructive thoughtfulness for the future.
Let the past sleep, but let it sleep on
the bosom of Christ. Leave the Irreparable Past
in His hands, and step out into
the Irresistible Future with Him.

—

Oswald Chambers

POINTS OF EMPHASIS:
Write Down at Least Three Things About Eternal Perspective That Your Son Needs to Hear from You:

_____

_____

_____

_____

_____

_____

_____

_____

_____

_____

_____

_____

_____

_____

_____

A TIME TO PRAY:
Write Down Your Prayer for Your Son about This Chapter:

Dear Lord,

_____

_____

_____

_____

_____

_____

_____

_____

_____

_____

_____

_____

_____

_____

Amen

THE FACT THAT YOU ENCOUNTER TOUGH TIMES IS NOT NEARLY AS IMPORTANT AS THE WAY YOU CHOOSE TO DEAL WITH THEM.

God blesses the people who patiently endure testing.
Afterward they will receive the crown of life
that God has promised to those who love him.

James 1:12 NLT

TALK TO YOUR SON ABOUT OVERCOMING TOUGH TIMES

Every human life (including your son's) is a tapestry of events: some grand, some not-so-grand, and some downright disheartening. When your child reaches the mountaintops of life, he'll find that praising God is easy. But, when the storm clouds form overhead and he finds himself in the dark valleys of life, his faith will be stretched, sometimes to the breaking point.

As Christians, we can be comforted: Wherever we find ourselves, whether at the top of the mountain or the depths of the valley, God is there, and because He cares for us, we can live courageously.

The Bible promises this: tough times are temporary but God's love is not—God's love lasts forever. Psalm 147 promises, "He heals the brokenhearted and binds up their wounds" (v. 3, Holman CSB), but Psalm 147 doesn't say that He heals them instantly. Usually, it takes time (and effort) to fix things.

So your son should learn that when he faces tough times, he should face them with God by his side. Your son should understand that when he encounters setbacks— and he will—he should always ask for God's help. And your son should learn to be patient. God will work things out, just as He has promised, but He will do it in His own way and in His own time.

I called to the Lord in my distress;
I called to my God.
From His temple He heard my voice.

—

2 Samuel 22:7 Holman CSB

MORE GREAT IDEAS

The sermon of your life in tough times ministers to people more powerfully than the most eloquent speaker.

Bill Bright

Sometimes we get tired of the burdens of life, but we know that Jesus Christ will meet us at the end of life's journey. And, that makes all the difference.

Billy Graham

God allows us to experience the low points of life in order to teach us lessons that we could learn in no other way.

C. S. Lewis

Our loving God uses difficulty in our lives to burn away the sin of self and build faith and spiritual power.

Bill Bright

We can stand affliction better than we can stand prosperity, for in prosperity we forget God.

D. L. Moody

Life will be made or broken at the place where we meet and deal with obstacles.

E. Stanley Jones

People who inspire others
are those who see invisible bridges
at the end of dead-end streets.

—

Charles Swindoll

POINTS OF EMPHASIS:
Write Down at Least Three Things About Adversity That
Your Son Needs to Hear from You:

_____

_____

_____

_____

_____

_____

_____

_____

_____

_____

_____

_____

_____

A TIME TO PRAY:
Write Down Your Prayer for Your Son about This Chapter:

Dear Lord,

_____

_____

_____

_____

_____

_____

_____

_____

_____

_____

_____

_____

_____

Amen

IT'S MORE DANGEROUS OUT THERE THAN YOU THINK, SO SLOW DOWN, BUCKLE UP, KEEP YOUR EYES ON THE ROAD, AND DON'T BE IMPULSIVE (WHETHER YOU'RE IN A CAR OR NOT).

The sensible see danger and take cover;
the foolish keep going and are punished.

–

Proverbs 27:12 Holman CSB

TALK TO YOUR SON ABOUT SAFETY

I t's a nightmare that, from time to time, crosses the mind of every loving parent: the thought that serious injury might befall a child. These parental fears are reinforced by tragic accidents that, all too often, are splashed across the headlines of our local newspapers.

Since no one can deny that far too many young people behave recklessly, it's your job, as a responsible parent, to do everything within your power to ensure that your child is far more safety conscious than the norm. In short, you should become your family's safety advisor. You should be vocal, you should be persistent, you should be consistent, and you should be informed.

Maturity and safety go hand in hand. So, as your son becomes a more mature young man, he'll naturally, if gradually, acquire the habit of looking before he leaps. And that's good because when young people leap first and look second, they often engage in destructive behavior that they soon come to regret.

So don't hesitate to talk to your son about safety, don't hesitate to teach him safe behavior, don't hesitate to plan for his safety, and, when necessary, don't hesitate to limit his access to people and places that might cause him physical, emotional, or spiritual harm.

Being a strict, safety-conscious parent may not be the quickest path to parental popularity. But it's one of the best things you can do to help your son enjoy a long, happy, productive life.

———•◆•———

The one who acquires good sense loves himself;
one who safeguards understanding finds success.
Proverbs 19:8 Holman CSB

Follow my advice, my son; always treasure my commands.
Obey them and live! Guard my teachings as your most
precious possession. Tie them on your fingers as a reminder.
Write them deep within your heart.
Proverbs 7:1-3 NLT

Even zeal is not good without knowledge,
and the one who acts hastily sins.
Proverbs 19:2 Holman CSB

MORE GREAT IDEAS

Sometimes, being wise is nothing more than slowing down long enough to think about things before you do them.

Jim Gallery

If we neglect the Bible, we cannot expect to benefit from the wisdom and direction that result from knowing God's Word.

Vonette Bright

When you and I are related to Jesus Christ, our strength and wisdom and peace and joy and love and hope may run out, but His life rushes in to keep us filled to the brim. We are showered with blessings, not because of anything we have or have not done, but simply because of Him.

Anne Graham Lotz

Wisdom is knowledge applied. Head knowledge is useless on the battlefield. Knowledge stamped on the heart makes one wise.

Beth Moore

The more wisdom enters our
hearts, the more we will be
able to trust our hearts
in difficult situations.

—

John Eldredge

TALKING TO YOUR SON ABOUT HEALTH

God intends that we take special care of the bodies He has given us. But it's tempting to do otherwise. We live in a fast-food world where unhealthy choices are convenient, inexpensive, and tempting. And, we live in a digital world filled with modern conveniences that often rob us of the physical exercise needed to maintain healthy lifestyles. As a result, too many of us, adults and children alike, find ourselves glued to the television, with a snack in one hand and a clicker in the other. The results are as unfortunate as they are predictable.

As adults, each of us bears a personal responsibility for the general state of our own physical health. Certainly, various aspects of health are beyond our control: illness sometimes strikes even the healthiest people. But for most of us, physical health is a choice: it is the result of hundreds of small decisions that we make every day of our lives. If we make decisions that promote good health, our bodies respond. But if we fall into bad habits and undisciplined lifestyles, we suffer tragic consequences.

When our unhealthy habits lead to poor health, we find it all too easy to look beyond ourselves and assign blame. In fact, we live in a society where blame has become a national obsession: we blame cigarette manufacturers, restaurants, and food producers, to name only a few.

But to blame others is to miss the point. We, and we alone, are responsible for the way that we treat our bodies. And the sooner that we accept that responsibility, the sooner we can assert control over our bodies and our lives.

Do you sincerely desire to improve your physical health? And do you wish to encourage your child to do likewise? If so, start by taking personal responsibility for the body that God has given you. Next, be sure to teach your son the common-sense lessons of sensible diet and regular exercise. Then, make a solemn pledge to yourself that you'll help your family make the choices that are necessary to enjoy longer, healthier, happier lives. No one can make those choices for you; you must make them for yourself. And with God's help, you can . . . and you will.

Don't you know that you are God's sanctuary and that the Spirit of God lives in you?

—

1 Corinthians 3:16 Holman CSB

MORE GREAT IDEAS

God wants you to give Him your body. Some people do foolish things with their bodies. God wants your body as a holy sacrifice.

Warren Wiersbe

The key to healthy eating is moderation and managing what you eat every day.

John Maxwell

Ultimate healing and the glorification of the body are certainly among the blessings of Calvary for the believing Christian. Immediate healing is not guaranteed.

Warren Wiersbe

You can't buy good health at the doctor's office—you've got to earn it for yourself.

Marie T. Freeman

People are funny. When they are young, they will spend their health to get wealth. Later, they will gladly pay all they have trying to get their health back.

John Maxwell

POINTS OF EMPHASIS:
Write Down at Least Three Things About Safety That Your Son Needs to Hear from You:

_____

_____

_____

_____

_____

_____

_____

_____

_____

_____

_____

_____

_____

A TIME TO PRAY:
Write Down Your Prayer for Your Son about This Chapter:

Dear Lord,

_____

_____

_____

_____

_____

_____

_____

_____

_____

_____

_____

_____

_____

Amen

JESUS OFFERS THE GIFT ETERNAL LIFE, AND THE REST IS UP TO YOU.

"I assure you: Anyone who hears My word and believes Him who sent Me has eternal life and will not come under judgment, but has passed from death to life."

John 5:24–25 Holman CSB

TALK TO YOUR SON ABOUT
ETERNAL LIFE

Eternal life is not an event that begins when we die. Eternal life begins when we invite Jesus into our hearts. The moment we allow Jesus to reign over our hearts, we've already begun our eternal journeys.

As a thoughtful Christian parent, it's important to remind your child that God's plans are not limited to the ups and downs of everyday life. In fact, the ups and downs of the daily grind are, quite often, impossible for us to understand. As mere mortals, our understanding of the present and our visions for the future—like our lives here on earth—are limited. God's vision is not burdened by such limitations: His plans extend throughout all eternity. And we must trust Him even when we cannot understand the particular details of His plan.

So let us praise the Creator for His priceless gift, and let us share the Good News with all who cross our paths. We return our Father's love by accepting His grace and by sharing His message and His love. When we do, we are blessed here on earth and throughout all eternity.

More from God's Word About Eternal Life

And this is the testimony: God has given us eternal life, and this life is in His Son. The one who has the Son has life. The one who doesn't have the Son of God does not have life.

1 John 5:11-12 Holman CSB

Jesus said to her, "I am the resurrection and the life. The one who believes in Me, even if he dies, will live. Everyone who lives and believes in Me will never die—ever. Do you believe this?"

John 11:25-26 Holman CSB

Pursue righteousness, godliness, faith, love, endurance, and gentleness. Fight the good fight for the faith; take hold of eternal life, to which you were called and have made a good confession before many witnesses.

1 Timothy 6:11-12 Holman CSB

I have written these things to you who believe in the name of the Son of God, so that you may know that you have eternal life.

1 John 5:13 Holman CSB

MORE GREAT IDEAS

And because we know Christ is alive, we have hope for the present and hope for life beyond the grave.

Billy Graham

Someday you will read in the papers that Moody is dead. Don't you believe a word of it. At that moment I shall be more alive than I am now. I was born of the flesh in 1837, I was born of the spirit in 1855. That which is born of the flesh may die. That which is born of the Spirit shall live forever.

D. L. Moody

Let us see the victorious Jesus, the conqueror of the tomb, the one who defied death. And let us be reminded that we, too, will be granted the same victory.

Max Lucado

Slowly and surely, we learn the great secret of life, which is to know God.

Oswald Chambers

God did not spring forth from eternity; He brought forth eternity.

C. H. Spurgeon

God's salvation comes as gift; it is eternal, and it is a continuum, meaning it starts when I receive the gift in faith and is never-ending.

Franklin Graham

Turn your life over to Christ today, and your life will never be the same.

Billy Graham

Once a man is united to God, how could he not live forever? Once a man is separated from God, what can he do but wither and die?

C. S. Lewis

The damage done to us on this earth will never find its way into that safe city. We can relax, we can rest, and though some of us can hardly imagine it, we can prepare to feel safe and secure for all of eternity.

Bill Hybels

POINTS OF EMPHASIS:
Write Down at Least Three Things About Eternal Life
That Your Son Needs to Hear from You:

_____

_____

_____

_____

_____

_____

_____

_____

_____

_____

_____

_____

_____

_____

A Time to Pray:
Write Down Your Prayer for Your Son about This Chapter:

Dear Lord,

_____

_____

_____

_____

_____

_____

_____

_____

_____

_____

_____

_____

_____

Amen

Then an argument started among them
about who would be the greatest of them.
But Jesus, knowing the thoughts of their hearts,
took a little child and had him
stand next to Him. He told them,
"Whoever welcomes this little child in My name
welcomes Me. And whoever welcomes Me
welcomes Him who sent Me.
For whoever is least among you all—
this one is great."

—

Luke 9:46-48 Holman CSB